...ENTIONS

Toys and Games

Jane Bidder

W
FRANKLIN WATTS
LONDON•SYDNEY

This edition 2009

Franklin Watts
338 Euston Road
London NW1 3BH

Franklin Watts Australia
Hachette Children's Books
Level 17/207 Kent Street
Sydney NSW 2000

Series editor: Jennifer Schofield
Designer: Ross George
Picture researcher: Diana Morris
Artwork: Ray Bryant
Photography: Ray Moller unless otherwise acknowledged

Acknowledgements:
With special thanks to Mattel Inc for supplying
Polly Pocket and Matchbox and Hot Wheels cars.

The author would like to thank Mary Bellis
of http://inventors.about.com for her help in researching this book.

Antikensammlung, Staatliche Museen, Berlin/Bildarchiv Preussischer Kulturbesitz: 12b;
Sarah Fabian-Baddiel/HIP/Topfoto: 21; The British Library, London: 5br, 10b; British Pathé/
ITN Stills: 19t; Sally Chappel/V & A Museum, London/Art Archive: 16bl. Christies Images:
front cover tl; The Computer History Museum, Ca, USA: 24b; Duncan Toys: 13b; Mary Evans
Picture Library: 22b, 26t; Malcolm Case-Green/Alamy: 24t; Keystone/Topfoto: 25; The National
Yo Yo Museum & Contest, Ca, USA. All rights reserved: 12t; Nicholas Sapieha, Poggio Petroio
Dog Collection/Art Archive: 3br, 10t; Sothebys/AKG Images: 7tr; Tamiya/The Hobby Company
2005; www.tamiya.com: 19b; Michael Teller/AKG Images: 20b; Yves Tzaud/Photographers
Direct: 23; John Warren/Topfoto: 8b; Karl Weatherly/ Corbis: 22t; Jerome Yeats/Alamy: 18.

Every attempt has been made to clear copyright.
Should there be any inadvertent omission please
apply to the publisher for rectification.

A CIP catalogue record for this book
is available from the British Library.

ISBN 978 0 7496 8950 6
Dewey Classification: 790.1'33

Printed in China

Franklin Watts is a division of Hachette Children's Books,
an Hachette UK company.
www.hachette.co.uk

Contents

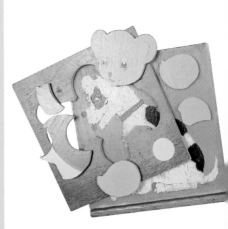

About inventions

An invention is a device or a gadget that is designed and made for the first time. The person who makes the device is called an inventor. In this book, we look at some of the playful inventions that keep us entertained. We will also investigate who invented them and how they have changed over time.

Making life fun

Many toys and games have been invented to help people to relax. The game of chess has been played around the world since 700 CE. Although chess is a game of tactics and you have to concentrate to play it, it is an enjoyable way to spend time with a friend.

From one comes another

Many inventions change and develop from earlier ideas or are improved over time. For example, in 100 CE yo-yos were made from terracotta, which is a heavy clay. Then, much later, in 1400 CE wooden yo-yos were made. Today, most yo-yos are made from plastic. Some even have lights that glow as the yo-yos move up and down.

Learning through play

Many toys were invented to teach children about the adult world, or to help with their education. Map puzzles teach children geography while many board games really make you think! Some toys help you to make up stories in your head. Until the last 200 years, most toys were made from materials found easily around the house.

T I M E L I N E S

You will find timelines throughout this book. They show in date order when a specific breakthrough or invention occurred.

Sometimes the dates are very exact, but other times they point to a particular historical era or decade, for example the 1990s.

Use these timelines to keep track of when things happened.

Teddy bears

Teddy bears have not changed much since they were first made over 100 years ago. Today, these cuddly toys are still popular with both adults and children.

Going hunting

In 1902, Theodore (Teddy) Roosevelt, the US President, went hunting. When he refused to shoot a bear cub, the story appeared in a newspaper, showing a cartoon of the president sparing the cub's life. A shopkeeper called Morris Mitchom saw the cartoon and his wife made a soft toy bear, with black buttons for eyes, to put in their shop window. Morris put a sign next to it, saying 'Teddy's Bear'. By 1907, most soft toy bears made in Europe and the USA were called teddy bears.

Steiff bears

Also in 1902, the German toy company, Steiff, made the first toy bear that had jointed arms and legs. It was shown at the Leipzig Toy Fair in 1903. The bear was spotted by an American shopowner who ordered 3,000 Steiff bears to sell back home.

Winnie-the-Pooh

In 1921, Christopher Robin Milne was given a teddy bear for his first birthday. His father, the English author AA Milne, saw how his son loved playing with his bear and decided to write a story about a boy, his teddy bear and other toys. In 1925, *Winnie-the-Pooh* was published. Today, Winnie-the-Pooh remains one of the world's best-known teddy bears.

TIMELINE

1902
Morris Mitchom puts 'Teddy's Bear' in his shop window.

1902
The Steiff toy company makes jointed toy bears to sell at a toy fair. Soon everyone wants a teddy bear.

1920
Teddy bears wearing clothes are made.

1925
Winnie-the-Pooh is published. It is followed by *The House at Pooh Corner.*

1997
The first Build-a-Bear Workshop store is opened in St Louis, USA. At these stores, children can choose, make and dress their own bears.

Board games

Although there are many new and exciting board games available today, some of the most popular games, such as chess and draughts, were invented hundreds, or even thousands, of years ago.

Snakes and Ladders

Snakes and Ladders developed from an ancient Indian game called Moksha-Patamu. The game became popular in England in 1892. It is thought that the game was invented

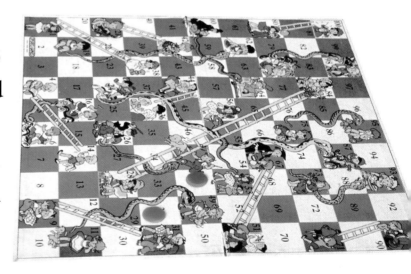

to teach people about good and bad. Moving up a ladder is like doing good because it helps you to go up in life, but going down a snake is like doing something bad because you fall back.

Draughts

The game of draughts probably developed from an Egyptian game called Alquerque, around 600 BCE. It was originally played on stone slabs until someone thought to use a wooden chess board, in around 1100 CE. In the 1600s, the French took to the game, but called it Jeu Force. In the USA it is called checkers.

Chess

No one is certain when chess was invented but it was played in the 8th century in India and in Persia (now Iran). By the 11th century, chess was played in Britain and records show that England's King Canute played it, too. Legend goes that after arguing during a game, he had his opponent killed.

T I M E L I N E

600 BCE
Draughts is played in Ancient Egypt.

700 CE
Chess is invented in India and quickly spreads to Persia (now Iran).

900s
Chess comes to Europe.

1600s
The French adopt draughts.

1892
Snakes and Ladders becomes popular in England.

1980s
Computer chess games are available.

Jigsaw puzzles

In the shops, you can find jigsaw puzzles for all ages and interests. But have you ever wondered who first had the idea of cutting up a picture that could be joined back together again?

Map puzzles

In 1767, a London mapmaker called John Spilsbury put one of his maps on a large piece of wood and cut around the outside of each country with a saw. He did this so children could learn to piece the countries together to make a map of the world.

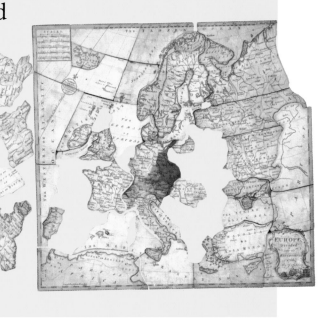

More pictures

At first, jigsaw puzzles were a learning tool. But by 1880, pictures other than maps were being glued onto wood and then cut out with saws. By about 1890, puzzles were made out of cardboard as well as wood. Then, in the 1920s and 1930s, companies like Chad Valley in Britain and Einson-Freeman in the USA began making lots of different kinds of jigsaw puzzles.

Keeping busy

In 1932, during the Great Depression in the USA, a weekly jigsaw puzzle was made and sold like a magazine. At first only 12,000 puzzles were made each week but it soon caught on as a way to pass time cheaply. At one point, puzzle-makers were making up to 200,000 puzzles a week!

TIMELINE

1767
John Spilsbury makes map puzzles.

1880
Pictures other than maps are used for the puzzles.

1890
Jigsaws are made out of cardboard, as well as wood.

1920s–30s
Companies begin mass-producing jigsaw puzzles on a weekly basis.

Late 1950s
Three-dimensional puzzles are made. Instead of building a flat puzzle, the puzzle stands upright.

Yo-yos

It takes a bit of practice to master the yo-yo, but once you get the hang of it, yo-yos are great fun. Some people enter competitions to show off their yo-yo tricks.

Yo-yo fun
In the late 18th century, the French Emperor Napoleon is said to have enjoyed playing with yo-yos to relax.

Ancient yo-yos

Historians think that the yo-yo is one of the oldest toys in the world. In fact, you can see ancient yo-yos, probably made from clay, in pictures found on Ancient Greek artefacts.

Wooden yo-yos

The first wooden yo-yos were made in the Philippines and from the 1400s onwards, they became popular in Africa and Europe. Like many toys, early yo-yos were made by parents for their children.

Donald Duncan's yo-yo company

In 1929, Donald Duncan, from the USA, bought a yo-yo company. He made some improvements to the yo-yo design and then decided to start making yo-yos out of plastic. They were lighter and easier to use. Duncan also sent his staff around the USA to show people how to do yo-yo tricks, creating a yo-yo craze as they went.

T I M E L I N E

100 CE
Yo-yos are used in Ancient Greece.

1400s
Yo-yos are made of wood. They become popular all around the world.

1800s
English children start playing with yo-yos.

1950s
Plastic yo-yos are made by Donald Duncan's company.

1990s
A yo-yo craze sweeps England.

Miniature cars

Miniature cars look just like real cars, only smaller. They have been popular for many years and some people collect them.

Dinky cars

In the early 1900s, the first miniature car, a Model T Ford, was made in the USA by Dowst Brothers Company. Later, in 1931 in Britain, miniature cars were made by Frank Hornby of Meccano Ltd. His company already sold toy train sets (see page 23) so the miniature cars, plus planes and lorries, completed the set. They were called Dinky toys.

'Dink' Dinky
The Dinky toy name is said to have come from the Scottish word, 'dink', meaning 'cute' or 'neat'.

Real cars, only smaller

In the 1950s, a company called Lesney started making Matchbox cars. Matchbox cars were miniature copies of the cars driving along the roads. Many children, and even adults, began collecting them.

Very Hot Wheels

In 1968, a new kind of miniature car came along. It was made by the US toy company Mattel and was called Hot Wheels. These cars were made with low-friction wheels, which meant that they could move faster and further than other toy cars.

TIMELINE

Early 1900s
Dowst Brothers Company makes a miniature Model T.

1931
Frank Hornby designs Dinky toys.

1950s
Matchbox cars appear in shops.

1958
Scalextric, an electric racing car toy that drives on a track, is invented.

1960s
Mattel's Hot Wheels cars start to be popular.

2000s
Miniature cars are still popular and are traded on-line.

Dolls

Dolls come in all shapes and sizes. Some look just like real babies while others are like fashion models. Children have played with dolls for at least 4,000 years. Over time, dolls have been made from rags, wood, wax, china, rubber and plastic, like modern Polly Pocket.

Queen Anne dolls

In the 1600s, many children played with simple wooden dolls. At this time, a special kind of doll was made, known as a 'Queen Anne' doll after the queen of the day. It had splendid dolls' clothes and jointed legs but was made for adults, not children.

China dolls

From the 1840s, many doll-makers started creating china heads, legs and arms for their dolls. In fact, the heads were often sold separately so that the child could choose which head they wanted for their new doll. The china could break so children played carefully with their dolls.

Polly Pocket

In 1983, an Englishman called Chris Wiggs designed a small doll for his daughter. Six years later, the first Polly Pocket appeared in the shops. These tiny plastic dolls with removable clothes are now made by the toy company Mattel.

TIMELINE

2000 BCE
Egyptian children play with cloth dolls.

1200 CE
Children have wooden dolls.

1600s
Wooden dolls are made with limbs.

1700s
Dolls are made of wax.

1840s
Dolls are made with soft fabric bodies and china arms, legs and heads.

1900s
Dolls are made of all kinds of materials, including plastic.

1959
Barbie is invented.

1989
The first Polly Pocket doll goes on sale.

Radio-controlled toys

A radio-controlled toy is a model toy, such as an aeroplane, car or boat, that is controlled by a radio transmitter. The transmitter is held by someone at a distance away from the toy so that it appears to move on its own.

Super quick!
Some models run on nitromethane, or nitro for short. This is the same as the fuel used by real dragsters and some racing cars.

Radio-controlled boats

In 1898, a scientist named Nikola Tesla held a public demonstration of the first radio-controlled boat in New York, USA. The steering and propulsion on Tesla's boat could be controlled by radio technology. Today, radio-controlled boats remain popular toys for children and adults alike.

First flight

The first officially recorded model aeroplane flight was made by Britain's Colonel 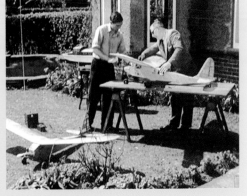 HJ Taplin in 1957. Colonel Taplin created the plane himself.

Spin dizzies

Radio-controlled cars were first made in the 1940s but as the cars could move only in circles, they were called 'spin dizzies'. Then, in 1974, a Japanese company, called Tamiya, started selling models that moved in straight lines, too. This started a new toy craze.

TIMELINE

1898
Nikola Tesla gives a demonstration of a radio-controlled boat.

1940s
The first radio-controlled cars appear.

1957
The first radio-controlled aeroplane flight is made by the UK's Colonel Taplin.

1974
Tamiya launches a radio-controlled M4 Sherman Tank, starting a new craze for radio-controlled toys.

1976
Tamiya launches a radio-controlled Porche 934.

2005
Tomy launches a new Herbie the Beetle remote-controlled car to tie in with the film.

Train sets

Soon after steam trains were invented in the 1840s, people invented toy trains for children. They were made from wood and children pushed them across the floor, or pulled them along with string. Today, train sets are made from plastic or metal and use electricity to move about.

Magical Marklin

In 1891, a German toy company called Marklin started selling toy trains and the tracks to go with them. At first the Marklin trains were driven by clockwork, then they were powered by steam. The steam trains were expensive, so only the children of wealthy parents owned them.

Lionel trains

In 1900, the American Joshua Lionel Cowen formed a toy company making trains. The company, called Lionel, still operates today. One of its most recent developments is called RailSounds II which reproduces the actual sounds that trains make.

Frank Hornby's trains

In Britain and France, Frank Hornby's Meccano Ltd led the way in developing electric train sets in the 1920s. They were sold alongside existing clockwork models. Over the next 30 years, electric train sets became popular. Children could buy carriages, figures and other items to go with their train set.

TIMELINE

1840s
The first toy trains are made of wood.

1870s
Trains that move by clockwork or steam are sold.

1891
Marklin makes toy trains with tracks.

1900
Lionel Manufacturing Company forms.

1920s
Electric toy trains become popular.

1935
Lionel makes the first train with a whistle sound.

1938
Hornby's Dublo train is sold in clockwork or electric form.

1994
Lionel trains that reproduce train noises are sold.

Skateboards

Skateboards may be quite a recent toy invention, but they are one of the most popular. While many people skateboard for fun, skateboarding is also taken seriously as a sport around the world, with both adults and children taking part.

Skateboarding starts

In 1760, Belgium-born Jean-Joseph Merlin made the first rollerskates. Nearly 150 years later, in the early 1900s, people began fixing rollerskate wheels onto pieces of wood.

Keep covered!
Skateboarders' safety has become more important. Today, boarders wear helmets and sometimes knee and elbow pads, too.

Surfing the streets

Skateboarding really took off in the early 1960s when Larry Stevenson of the USA got people to use skateboards to surf the streets. Then, in 1963, his company, 'Mahaka', made the first professional skateboards. Within just a few years, over 50 million skateboards were sold.

All about wheels

The early skateboards had wheels made from clay. These did not grip surfaces very well and many skateboarders had bad accidents. However, in 1973, another American, Frank Nasworthy, introduced plastic wheels which made skateboards much safer.

TIMELINE

1760
Merlin makes the first rollerskates.

Early 1900s
People fit rollerskate wheels onto wood to make skateboards.

1963
The first professional boards are made by the Mahaka company.

1973
Frank Nasworthy designs a plastic wheel which makes skateboards much safer.

1976
The first skateboard park is built in Florida, USA.

1993
The first X Games takes place. These are like the Olympics of extreme sports, including skateboarding.

Computer games

Computer games may be one of the newest toys that we have today, but even they have changed in how they look. They certainly were not as popular when they first appeared.

Warning!
Always check the age rating on computer games and ask an adult for permission before you start playing a computer game.

Spacewar

The first computer game was called Spacewar. It was invented by three American scientists called Russell, Samson and Graetz in 1962. The aim of Spacewar was for spaceships to shoot at each other.

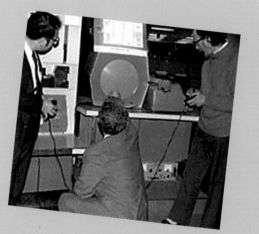

In your hands!

In 1989, hand-held games consoles, such as Game Boy, were invented by Nintendo. One of the most popular games to play was Tetris, where players had to pack different coloured shapes into a grid.

Through the television

Since the 1980s, lots of games and home consoles have been made, many of which use the television screen. These include the Sony Playstation in 2000 and the Microsoft Xbox, launched in 2001. In 2005, the hand-held Sony Playstation was launched (see above). It is small enough to fit in backpacks and briefcases and it can be played with headphones.

1962
Spacewar is invented.

1974
The tennis game, Pong, becomes available for home use.

1980
Pac-Man is launched by Nintendo.

1989
Game Boy consoles and Tetris go on sale.

1994
CD-ROM games for home computers become popular.

2000
Playstation One is made by the Sony Corporation.

2001
Microsoft Xbox is launched.

2005
A portable Playstation is launched by Sony.

Other inventions

There are many other toys and games that people play with. Some were invented such a long time ago that we do not know the inventor. Building blocks, kites and skipping ropes fall into this group.

Building blocks

Children have played with building blocks for hundreds of years. At first, children used stones as building blocks but later, in the Victorian era, blocks were made from wood. Today, there is a huge variety of building toys, from plastic Lego and K'nex to magnetic Geomags.

Kites

It is thought that kites were invented by the Chinese 3,000 years ago. They were made out of silk and bamboo. Today, there are many different kinds of kite, such as stunt kites and huge kites for kite-surfing. Some of today's kites have nylon sails fixed to fibre-glass frames.

Skipping ropes

Skipping has been popular since the 1800s. Then, skipping ropes had wooden handles and many children played complicated skipping games with friends. Although some of today's ropes also have wooden handles, most are now plastic.

Plastic is one of the most common materials for making toys – without it, many of the toys in this book would not be possible.

Plastic is used to make toys because it is tough, safe, waterproof, easily moulded and it can be brightly coloured.

Plastic was accidentally discovered by two chemists, J Paul Hogan and Robert L Banks. While the chemists were trying to make fuel, they realised that their equipment had become clogged up with a sticky, white substance. They recreated the white substance and realised that it was a new material.

Timeline

2000 BCE
Egyptian children play with cloth dolls, marbles, spinning tops and pull-along toys.

700 CE
Chess is played in India and Persia (Iran).

1200 CE
Children have wooden dolls.

1400s
Yo-yos are made of wood.

1600s
Jointed dolls are invented.

1700s
Dolls are made of wax.

1767
John Spilsbury makes the first jigsaw puzzle.

1840s
The first toy trains are made from wood.

1870s
Trains are made out of tin and are moved by clockwork or steam.

1890
Jigsaws are made out of cardboard, as well as wood.

1892
Snakes and Ladders becomes popular in England.

1898
Nikola Tesla demonstrates a radio-controlled boat.

Early 1900s
The first skateboards are made.

1902
Morris Mitchom displays a 'Teddy's bear' in his shop.

1929
Donald Duncan buys a yo-yo company.

1931
Dinky cars appear.

1950s
Matchbox makes miniature cars.

1957
A radio-controlled plane flies.

1959
The Barbie doll is invented.

1960s
Hot Wheels friction cars start to be popular.

1962
The first computer game, Spacewar, is invented in the USA.

1974
The video game, Pong, is launched for home use.

1989
The first Polly Pocket doll goes on sale.

1989
Game Boy consoles go on sale. The game Tetris becomes very popular.

2000
Playstation One is made by the Sony Corporation.

2001
Microsoft Xbox is launched.

Glossary

Clay
A material found in the Earth that hardens when it is heated. Clay can be moulded and hardened to make many things.

Clockwork
The way a toy train is powered or made to move. This could be by weights pulling down or coiled-up springs slowly unwinding.

Consoles
The main part of a computer game in which the operating system is found.

Craze
When a toy is in fashion, it is the latest craze.

Fibreglass
A material made up of very fine fibres of glass.

Great Depression
The time from 1929 through the 1930s when the USA lost a lot of money and people were poor.

Historians
People who study and write about history.

Low-friction wheels
Wheels with little resistance between them and the surface they are moving on. This means that the wheels can turn faster.

Patented
When someone owns the rights to an invention so that it cannot be copied by other inventors.

Plastic
A material used to make many toys. Plastic is waterproof and long-lasting.

Propulsion
When something is propelled or moved forwards.

Radio transmitter
A device that transfers radio waves from one machine or gadget to another.

Three-dimensional
Having three dimensions: length, width and height.

Victorian era
The time when Queen Victoria of England was on the throne, between 1837 and 1901.

Websites

**www.nationalgeographic.com/
features/96/inventions**
Have loads of fun with games about
inventions.

http://home.howstuffworks.com
Find out how everyday inventions
work by searching for them on this
website.

**www.uspto.gov/web/offices/ac/
ahrpa/opa/kids/index.html**
Visit the American Patent and
Trademark Office's website to find
out more about inventions and how
they are patented.

**www.hants.gov.uk/museum/toys/
history/toy_cars.html**
Explore the Hampshire Museum's great
collection of toys.

www.vam.ac.uk/moc
Visit the Museum of Childhood, for
a virtual tour of its collections.

**www.historychannel.com/
exhibits/toys/index.html**
Read all about your favourite
toys, who invented them and
how they work.

www.yo-yo.com
Find out all about Duncan yo-yos -
from the first models to the latest
yo-yo crazes. Click on 'multimedia'
for loads of fun yo-yo games,
downloads and art.

www.mattel.com/our_toys
Look at the websites of all your
favourite Mattel toys, including
Hot Wheels, Matchbox cars, Barbie
and Polly Pocket.

Note to parents:
Every effort has been made by the publishers
to ensure that the websites in this book are
suitable for children, that they are of the
highest educational value, and that they
contain no inappropriate or offensive
material. However, due to the nature of the
Internet, it is impossible to guarantee that
the contents of these sites will not be altered.
We strongly advise that Internet access
is supervised by a responsible adult.

Index